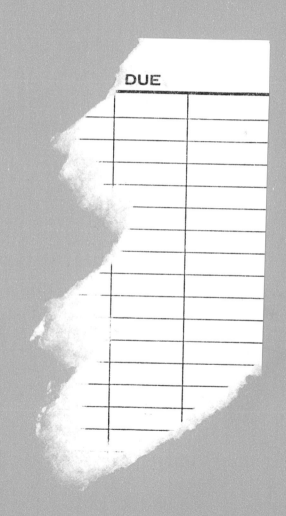

DUE

Gold Rush

GOLD RUSH

by

James Blower

Foreword by The Honourable Grant MacEwan
Lieutenant-Governor of Alberta

American Heritage Press New York

ISBN 0-07-092919-X

Library of Congress Catalog Card Number 70-156975

Published in the United States of America
by American Heritage Press,
a subsidiary of McGraw-Hill, Inc.

ISBN 0-07-092930-0

1 2 3 4 5 6 7 8 9 10 BP-71 0 9 8 7 6 5 4 3 2 1

Printed and bound in Canada

To my wife Linda
with love

FOREWORD

Canadians are showing an ever-increasing interest in their heritage – their history and their traditions as well as their more tangible resources. They are finding that even local history can be both useful and charming and it is reassuring to see the emergence of another chapter in the great story of a nation, this one, *Gold Rush*, presented in word and picture.

There should be no mistake about it: the search for the precious metal occupied a big place in pioneer thought and conversation. As Westerners of a later period might speak hopefully about striking oil or winning a sweepstake, the pioneers dreamed about making a major find in gold. They were familiar with the California Gold Rush and then the rush to the Upper Fraser River in British Columbia, and they expected further discoveries, perhaps nearer home.

As early as 1862, Thomas Clover travelled upriver from his prospecting in the Fraser Canyon and over the mountains to conduct his searching on the North Saskatchewan River, above Edmonton. In the next few years many others, equipped with "grizzlies," sluice boxes, dredges and flat-bottom pans followed to work the gravel bars both above and below Edmonton, hoping to find their fortune.

While the search was still a part of daily conversation in and about Edmonton, news of rich discoveries on certain Klondike creeks leaked out of the North. At first there was local interest without excitement because such rumors were fairly common and generally groundless. But when the reports from the North persisted, prospectors and would-be prospectors felt the urge to be going. At first the movement was like a trickle, then like a torrent. Most miners went by way of the coast and Skagway, but some chose the more direct – and more difficult – approach from Edmonton.

The overland route from Edmonton was an unwise choice and it led to more tragedies than fortunes. But the impact upon the Edmonton community was great. Outfitting merchants prospered and the town population doubled in two years. Regardless of the disappointments and losses experienced by those who elected to start from Edmonton, the town emerged as the new Gateway to the North, just as Winnipeg, because of the flood of immigrants coming that way, could claim to be the Gateway to the West. The Town of Edmonton – soon to become a city – exerted an important influence upon the North, just as the North exerted its magic influence upon the city. The story is one in which Canadians everywhere should find interest.

Grant MacEwan

Introduction

Although this is mainly a picture book, the accompanying text and the photo captions have also, for the most part, been taken from primary sources within the research materials of the Provincial Museum and Archives of Alberta. Until recently this material had gone virtually unnoticed, and as a result much of the information included here is published for the first time.

It is my sincere hope that this collection of photographs will help show to what extent the gold era helped shape the Edmonton region. The book deals both with the Edmonton gold mining efforts, and with the role Edmonton played in the Yukon gold rush of 1898.

Most of Alberta's early photographers have long since passed on, and unfortunately their work has followed. In early days all negatives were produced on glass plates, which rendered them extremely vulnerable to environmental conditions. The photographs in this book represent chiefly the work of two men: W. C. Mathers, Edmonton's first photographer, and Ernest Brown, his successor. The early photographs pertaining to Edmonton and the Far North are the work of Mr. Mathers, while those of Edmonton during its later stages of development are by Mr. Brown.

The first mention of gold in the Saskatchewan River came by way of the Palliser Expedition of 1857 to 1860. It was reported that, while investigating the settlement possibilities of the region now called Alberta, the Palliser party had found some traces of gold along the river's edge. As a result of this find a prospector from the Fraser Valley, Thomas Clover, decided to try his luck on the river and after a somewhat slow start he was able to settle down to work, in 1862, on a large sand bar just east of Fort Edmonton.

As time went on, the number of miners increased, and by 1894 the river was a beehive of activity, with the miners employing both manual and mechanical equipment in an effort to retrieve the Saskatchewan's gold. The boom lasted many years, and it was not until 1907 that the prospectors left the banks of the river for the last time.

However, what eventually brought most of the gold miners to the Edmonton area was not the gold of the Saskatchewan, but the discovery of large gold deposits in the Yukon Territories. In 1898 the news of the gold rush in the Yukon seemed far away and of little importance to many of the inhabitants of Edmonton; for this was by no means the first time they had heard the cry of gold from the north, and most felt it would not be the last.

The Klondike region had been prospected prior to 1886, and some gold taken from it, causing mild excitement in the immediate vicinity. However, in 1897 an Illinois man named George Carmack settled in the area after marrying a local Indian woman. While on a fishing trip with two of his friends he located a rich placer on what is now known as Bonanza Creek. With primitive tools Carmack was able to wash out over $1,200 worth of gold in a few days.

This find, and many similar ones during the following summer and late fall, started the stampede which quickly grew into the Klondike gold rush of '98 and resulted in a great northward wave of miners, many of whom passed through Edmonton on their way to the Yukon.

The trail to the Yukon from Edmonton was by no means easy, but then neither were any of the routes on the west coast used to reach the gold fields. The "Back Door Route," as it was called in its earlier days, did possess some advantages over the other routes. One of the main attractions of the trail was that, rather than lead the men over cold mountain passes, it travelled between the mountains by way of the river valleys, thus eliminating the worst hazard of all the overland routes.

As might be expected in a new and unexplored terrain, the route to the Klondike from Edmonton took its toll of men through drowning, starvation, scurvy and cold. Those that were strong enough to endure the hardships reached their destination; those that were weak, ill-prepared or foolhardy, perished.

For the Klondiker travelling from Edmonton, transportation northward came in every form and shape imaginable: from sleighs and dog teams in the winter months to burros and pack horses in the summer and late fall. Walter's Mill, situated on the south bank of the Saskatchewan River, produced many sleds and "jumpers" for those individuals heading into the northlands via Edmonton, and places as far away as Calgary sold horses to the would-be prospectors. At Athabasca Landing, north of Edmonton, river transportation was developing into a large business, and for many miles, both up and down the river one could see the new scows being constructed.

The rush of '98 brought many of Edmonton's merchants more money than they had ever hoped for. The gold in the North and in the Saskatchewan brought hordes of men from the United States and eastern Canada to the district, doubling the town's population and leaving behind well over $600,000, in exchange for supplies, in the pockets of the local merchants.

An excerpt from the Edmonton Bulletin of 1898 states:

As an outfitting point, Edmonton is the best and cheapest to outfit in for many reasons. We manufacture our own flour, the very best quality, also bacon and cured meats.

We know exactly the goods required and quantities needed. In many lines we get these goods in carloads, thus getting the very lowest freight rates. We carry very large stocks ordinarily to meet the requirements of our regular trade, but this season we are making specially large importations to meet the great demand there is sure to be.

Everything necessary for outfitting is carried in stock here, so that there is no need to bring anything with you. Edmonton can outfit all who come along.

Outside interest in both Edmonton and the Yukon grew, and companies of every description began to establish their claims on the land. Mining companies, gold dredging syndicates and exploration corporations were continually passing through town on their trek northward, or arriving with equipment for use on the Saskatchewan River. Names of large financial backers began appearing in the form of: "The Montreal Mining and Trade Company," "The Good Hope Mining and Development Corporation" and "The Northern Dredging Company."

Within a very short time smaller outfits also began appearing on the river, and men like Captain Abel Pearce of Nova Scotia began building and operating small hand powered dredges for local businessmen like Ed Lyons, an old-timer of the Edmonton District. For a number of seasons several small dredges were working the river, and their owners included such people as Frank Osborne, William McGee, Al Garley and the Denner Brothers. All of these dredges were very ingenious contraptions, the materials being collected from scrap piles and discarded machinery, but they all worked. They all earned considerably more than their expenses and some did much better than the larger and more elaborately equipped dredges built a few years later.

The roster of individuals responsible for the excitement generated during the gold era is long, and many descendants of these people still reside in Edmonton today. Looking through the old city records one finds such family names as: Nagle, Frazer, Braithwaite, Jenner, Potter, Huff, and many, many more. All of them played a large part in the development of this region during the 1890s.

It is said, a historical event need not be of worldwide importance in order to receive due recognition and honour. The only requirement is that it happen. Such was the case of Edmonton and the "days of golden opportunity": perhaps, on the overall scale very small, but nevertheless important to Edmonton's early history.

Trail to the Yukon

In 1897 the town of Edmonton, Northwest Territories, was just beginning to emerge from its infancy and boasted a population of approximately 1500 people. The newly elected mayor, The Honourable John A. McDougall, had just succeeded in obtaining the capital needed to construct the High Level Bridge over the Saskatchewan River, linking Edmonton with Strathcona. About this time land development began to boom and new settlers arrived in increasing numbers. All in all the outlook for Edmonton seemed to hold great promise for the future.

In the fall of 1897 the cry of gold in the North sent men from eastern Canada and the United States to the Yukon gold fields, using two main routes. The bulk of the Klondikers chose the Canadian west coast route, and reached the Yukon by way of steamer and inland trails, all of which led them over treacherous and slow-going mountain passes.

The alternative was the trail east of the Rocky Mountains through Edmonton, known originally as the "Back Door Route" and later officially as the "All Canadian Route." Since Edmonton was the largest and therefore best equipped town in the region it became the principal outfitting centre for those parties travelling this route to the gold fields. As a result of this influx of people the town's population doubled within two years.

From Edmonton's Main Street the prospectors, numbering two thousand, would wind their way northward by stage or wagon to Athabasca Landing. Once at the Landing they were able to procure river transportation in the form of Indian canoes, longboats, scows or river steamer.

The second step of the journey led them northward up the Athabasca River to Fort Chipewyan, and from there the prospectors crossed the tip of Lake Athabasca and entered the Slave River, which carried them to Fort Resolution on the shores of Great Slave Lake. The route then continued down the Mackenzie River, passed Fort Providence and Fort Good Hope, leaving behind many a slow and laborious portage overcome.

At the mouth of the Mackenzie Delta the prospectors entered the Peel River, which took them to the Canadian Rockies. Here they journeyed overland to the Steward River System, which opened the door to the Klondike gold fields.

The All Canadian Route followed the main river and lake systems used by the early fur traders and held the distinct advantage of having a number of Hudson's Bay Company trading posts set along the route, at which the prospectors were able to obtain additional supplies, or aid if needed.

There were many other excellent advantages afforded the men using the All Canadian Route, as opposed to the western coastal trails. It was first used because of the cheap source of food and mining supplies, as well as low priced pack horse transportation. The route also boasted a more moderate climate than any other trail, and this enabled the region to produce an abundance of feed for the animals throughout the entire length of the summer.

However, to many prospectors, the fact that the route passed down the river valleys, and not over the mountain passes like those of the west coast, afforded a sense of security – knowing they would not have to pack six hundred pounds of equipment over snowbound and ice-covered passes.

Some miners who left Edmonton chose an alternate route over the Assiniboine Trail, through the Swan Hills Wilderness area and up to the Peace River Country. From this point they travelled to the gold fields by way of the Pelly River. Unfortunately, this route presented numerous obstacles and, though many tried, few men completed the trip. The trail was littered with grave markers and discarded supplies.

Late in 1897 the Canadian Government, realizing the potential of the Yukon and the problems that were arising because of the congestion over the Chilkoot Pass and the All Canadian Route, began investigating the possibilities of a new trail. The major consideration would be its suitability for wagon and pack horse transportation.

In September of that year a party of men led by Inspector Moodie of the North West Mounted Police, accompanied by Constable Fitzgerald, F. Lafferty, R. Hardisty and an Indian guide named H. Tobin, set out from Edmonton in search of a new trail to the Klondike, via the Pelly River.

It was decided right from the start to follow the fur trade routes and intricate river systems from Edmonton through the Lesser Slave District, and by November the trail-blazing party had succeeded in reaching the Hudson's Bay Post of Fort St. John. Two months later they arrived at Fort Graham, where they prepared to wait out the remaining few months of the winter.

After resting at Fort Graham until spring, Inspector Moodie left for Quesnel in order to obtain additional supplies for the coming year, and by July the party was back at work on the Finlay River. When August of 1898 arrived the group had reached the Laird River, and by October their destination on the Pelly River was achieved, leaving only the last leg of the journey to Dawson City left to conquer. This portion of the trip was made by steamer.

By the time their trip was completed it had led them through dense muskeg, swamp lands and mosquito infested river bottoms, and had taken much longer than expected.

7

As a result of the conditions encountered by the men, Inspector Moodie, in his report, wrote: "With regards to the usefulness of the trail as a route to the Yukon, I should say it would never be used. . . ." So the All Canadian Route remained the primary passage to the gold fields from Edmonton.

The R.C.M.P. weren't the only ones interested in mapping new routes to and from the gold fields. There were those in the Yukon who were busily exploring the regions south and east of Dawson City in an attempt to discover a suitable route to civilization, one that could be developed into a wagon trail. The Edmonton *Bulletin* of 1897 gives this account concerning William Ogilvie, a government surveyor, who officially named the Back Door Route from Edmonton the All Canadian Route:

> The Yukon survey party is to be divided into three. One under W. Ogilvie is to go from Victoria, British Columbia, by steamer up the coast and reach the Yukon by Chilkoot Pass and Lewis River, the route taken by miners. Two parties will go into the Cassair country, whence one under Dr. Dawson will cross the Laird and the Pelly and descend the latter to the Yukon. The third under McConnell will go down the Laird to the Mackenzie and then follow the Hudson's Bay Company trade route to Winnipeg.

Others also tried to develop new routes and methods in hopes of monetary gain. One such group, under the direction of Dan Noyes, a prominent Edmontonian, founded the Alaska Mining and Transportation Company in 1898. Their idea was to supply the Klondikers with transportation in the form of a stage coach line from Edmonton to the Yukon. Like most schemes of that era, it never got off the ground.

How many men were able to reach their destination using the All Canadian Route will never be known. Most of the prospectors were not local residents, and communications in the North were such that when a man left Edmonton he was never heard from again, unless he happened to return to town at some later date. The trail held many hardships and as a rule only the strongest were able to survive the natural conditions of the terrain; and even some of these succumbed to the aroused Indians of the Beaver tribe, incensed at the miners who were destroying their traps and snares as well as driving out the wild game from the land.

Superintendent A. H. Griesbach, in his North West Mounted Police report for the year 1897 was quite concerned over the problems that seemed to be arising between the Indians and the prospectors, and made note of this fact to the government:

> The discovery of the rich gold fields in the Yukon and Peace River districts has given a great

impetus to business in Edmonton and vicinity, caused by the ever increasing numbers of people who are outfitting there and going into the north by this route.

In connection with this Yukon rush, I would observe that a great number of these travellers are of all countries and of a mixed class, and going as they are through an unorganized and Indian country, fully armed, trouble may ensue.

I would further point out that no treaties have been made with the Indians whose country these people are going through, and I am informed that they look with distrust on the influx of whites.

In view of these facts, I think that the sooner definite arrangements are made for the proper protection of this route by the establishment (about 400 miles north of Edmonton) of a police division with the attendant outposts, the better it will be.

George Carmack was the man responsible for sparking the Klondike Rush of '98. His rich placer mine on Bonanza Creek in the Yukon brought hundreds of men to the area in search of precious metals. "The Father of the Gold Rush" was pictured on the cover of the first issue of *The Klondike News*, Dawson, N.W.T., April 1st, 1898.

THE KLONDIKE NEWS

VOL I   DAWSON, N.W.T. APRIL 1ST, 1898.   NO. 1

OUTPUT FOR 1898 $40,000,000.

FROM Nº 8 EL DORADO.
PROPERTY OF CHAS. LAMB,
VALUE $315ᵀ⁰

SCHMIDT L. & LITH CO. S.F.

DISCOVERER.
GEO. W. CARMACK.

THE LARGEST GOLD NUGGET.
FOUND IN EL DORADO CREEK NO 36. BY M. KNUSTON
WEIGHT 36 OUNCES VALUE $530ᵀ⁰

William Ogilvie, a government surveyor and ex-commissioner of the Northwest Territories gave the "Back Door" Edmonton route to the Klondike the official title of the "All Canadian Route" – at no point did it pass through United States territory. The map shows the All Canadian Route as well as a lesser trail used by some miners, and also the North West Mounted Police trail-blazing detachment of 1897.

Wm. OGILVIE, ESQ.
Commissioner of Yukon Territory
1898 to 1901

ALL CANADIAN
AND
PELLY RIVER
ROUTES

Mackenzie
Delta

Great   Bear Lake

Yukon River

Peel River

○ FT. GOOD
HOPE

Dawson ○

Stewart   River

Mackenzie River

Great
Slave
Lake

Pelly River

FT.
PROVIDENCE
○

FT. RESOLUTION

Slave River

Athabasca
Lake

Nelson   River

FT. CHIPEWYAN

Peace River

Athabasca River

L. Slave River

ATHABASCA
LANDING   ○

EDMONTON   ○

Main Street, Edmonton, 1898 – outfitting point for the All Canadian Route north. Note the signs on Ross Bros. store offering Klondike supplies.

Individuals heading north would gather at Edmonton to form parties ranging from two or three men to forty or more. This photo was taken near what is now 100th Street and Jasper Avenue. In the background stands the old McDougall Church, and the wood frame structure behind the men is John A. McDougall's old store.

The All Canadian Route, unlike the coastal trails, was open year-round and "Klondikers," like the Glen Campbell party from Manitoba, would gather at Edmonton and head northward in both winter and summer. This photograph was taken at Edmonton's first race track, just north of what is now the Hudson's Bay Company Store.

The Leland party, like many others, camped on the banks of the Saskatchewan River while purchasing their supplies from the various merchants in Edmonton.

The Mason party, consisting of twenty-one men and twelve horse sleds, are shown on Jasper Avenue and approximately 105th Street, about to leave for the Yukon in the spring of '98.

With pack horses to carry them on the first step of their journey, this party left for the gold fields from the Groat Estate on the outskirts of Edmonton.

From Edmonton the prospectors travelled northward to Athabasca Landing, which was the starting point for the river travel to the gold fields. This photo shows Athabasca Landing, 1897.

At Athabasca Landing boat builders worked long hard hours in an effort to complete their craft – all were anxious to reach the Klondike. These men show a newly built scow, one of the most common types of boat used to navigate the northern rivers and lakes.

Klondikers built their boats along the banks of the Athabasca River, their supplies being sent via the town of Edmonton. This photo shows seven or eight scows near completion; in the background lies the Hudson's Bay Company steamer, the *Athabasca*.

At spring break-up, even before the ice floes had melted, the waters of the Athabasca were dotted with boats moving up to the Hudson's Bay post of Fort Chipewyan – all determined to reach the gold fields first.

Fort Chipewyan, on Athabasca Lake, saw many a Klondiker's craft pass by on its journey into the Slave River. The Fort, owned and operated by the Hudson's Bay Company, was one of the largest and most important stopping points for fur traders and prospectors alike, as supplies could always be replenished from the Bay's storehouses.

Just as the fur traders were forced to portage the countless numbers of rapids on the northern rivers, so did the miners. This photograph shows the last portage on the Slave River.

The Hudson's Bay Company's Fort Resolution was built on the shores of Great Slave Lake and served, like Fort Chipewyan, as a supply depot and resting point for the miners and trappers.

Many of the Klondikers never made it to the gold fields. Some died of starvation, others by drowning and a few from scurvy. This photograph shows a prospector's "scurvy shack," where a miner would go to recuperate – or to die in solitude.

Fort Providence, on the Mackenzie River, about forty miles below the outlet of Great Bear Lake, was built about 1850. This fort marked the beginning of the last large river system, the Mackenzie, en route to the Yukon and its gold.

Some prospectors travelled the Mackenzie River by way of Hudson's Bay steamers like the *Wrigley*. These steamers were normally used to carry supplies and equipment to the small settlements and outposts along the waterways.

The route from Edmonton to the Mackenzie Delta was approximately 1900 miles in length – if the weather held out and accidents were few, a man could complete the journey in about sixty-five days. During the rush, prospectors' camps were stretched from Edmonton up to the mouth of the Mackenzie and the Arctic Ocean.

Fort Good Hope was the most northerly post on the Mackenzie River – built on the right bank near the Mackenzie Delta. It was the last main stop for the prospectors before reaching the Arctic Ocean and the Yukon's Peel River.

Dawson City, Yukon, the end of the All Canadian Route and the hub of the Gold Rush. This photo shows Main Street, 1898.

In the winter months the North West Mounted Police employed the use of carioles or dog sleds to patrol the trails leading into the northlands – all waterways and inland routes were snowbound and travel by other means was slow and time consuming. The cariole was usually drawn by five dogs and on a good trail could make sixty miles in one day.

The men employed by the North West Mounted Police were of a special breed and stamina. This photograph shows the detachment of men designated to maintain peace and order in Edmonton during the early days of the gold rush.

54

In September 1897 North West Mounted Police Inspector John Douglas Moodie left Edmonton with a small detachment of men and headed northwest from Edmonton to the region known as the Pelly River. Their instructions read: "Find a new route to the Yukon, from Edmonton, suitable for wagon and pack horse travel." Although the men succeeded in mapping out the new trail, it was not until the Alaska Highway was constructed that their achievement was put to full use.

Superintendent A. H. Griesbach, commander of "G" Division for the North West Mounted Police, was a familiar figure during the early days of their work in the Northwest.

Although stationed at Fort Saskatchewan at the time of the gold rush, he was in charge of the entire area, including those forces later sent up the All Canadian Route to maintain law and order.

Transportation for the North

Down through the ages the lure of gold has always drawn men, and the rush of '98 was no exception. They came from eastern Canada, the United States, and even as far away as England and continental Europe. For when the gold fever struck, many men lost all sense of time and distance, their only concern being the wealth that lay at the end of their journey. Many times hardships were ignored or unprepared for, the result – disaster, and sometimes death.

Probably one of the best known stories of all regarding travel by greenhorns to the Klondike through Edmonton concerns a party of men from England, under the leadership of a Major Helpman. It is said that, tired and weary from their ocean voyage of over two thousand miles followed by two thousand miles of railway travel from the East, they finally reached Edmonton in the year 1897. Ignorant of what lay before them, one of the party, after stretching his legs on the station's loading platform, remarked: "Thank God the worst of the journey is over." How the party made out is not known, and all traces of their existence have, over the years, disappeared.

Cases like this were by no means rare, and were constantly cropping up during the gold rush years. One other story that comes to mind concerned a fellow in the United States who wrote to Edmonton asking if he could reach the gold fields by bicycle, using the route through Edmonton. Needless to say, his plans were drastically changed.

The intricacy of the American and Canadian railway systems, even in 1897, enabled many would-be prospectors to reach Edmonton with relatively little effort. Many of the railways south of the 49th parallel had direct contact with the Canadian Pacific, which spanned Canada from coast to coast, allowing miners to reach Edmonton from distant points throughout North America. The many Klondikers who used the railway travelled the Canadian Pacific's main route to Calgary, and from there booked passage for the remaining 180 miles northward to Edmonton and the start of the All Canadian Route.

Once in Edmonton, each miner would buy, build, or invent some means of transportation for his long trip of over sixteen hundred miles through thick forests and muddy swamps, over treacherous lakes and rivers to the gold-laden area in the Yukon. The route northward saw every type and mode of transportation available, from pack horses and ox teams to sleds and burros; and, since the trail led the prospectors through both land and water, river scows, sail boats and steamers played an important part in the story of transportation to the Klondike.

Throughout the winter of 1897, parties, some of as many as 44 men, left for the north from the outfitters' stores and headed down what is now Jasper Avenue, through St. Albert and up to Athabasca

Landing. In winter, with the use of dog sleds, "jumpers," horse drawn sleighs and pack trains, the parties could usually make quite good time by following the rivers, which were frozen over and free from obstructions.

In the summer months travel was somewhat slower but more comfortable, and the men would leave Edmonton by means of pack horses or wagons and travel to Athabasca Landing, where they would either build some type of sailing craft or travel the river by Hudson's Bay steam boats. One novel type of travel was tried by a Texan, who felt that empty whiskey barrels could quite easily be adapted to serve as a roller-type wagon, pulled by a team of horses. But unhappily his idea failed, and likewise his fortune.

In April 1898, a prominent businessman named John Gainer sold a steamboat to two men intent on reaching Dawson City from Edmonton by way of the river and lake systems. The craft was a vessel of some two and one-half tons burden and about forty feet in length, with a flat bottom. The power needed to propel the boat was supplied by a steam boiler attached to a stern wheel.

The two men, Jim Wallwork and Charles Roberts, began their voyage in early spring by sailing down the Saskatchewan River to a predesignated spot where they were to portage overland to Athabasca Landing. The portage was accomplished with the use of ox-teams and double wagons and, while the vessel was extremely cumbersome, it did reach the landing safely. Though many hardships and problems were encountered during the next few months, and the original partnership was dissolved, Jim Wallwork managed to reach Dawson City sixteen months later on July 9, 1899. All in all, the inventiveness and eagerness of the men touched the imagination of all concerned.

Various railway companies distributed maps, like this one published in 1898, showing the transportation routes to Edmonton from eastern Canada and the United States.

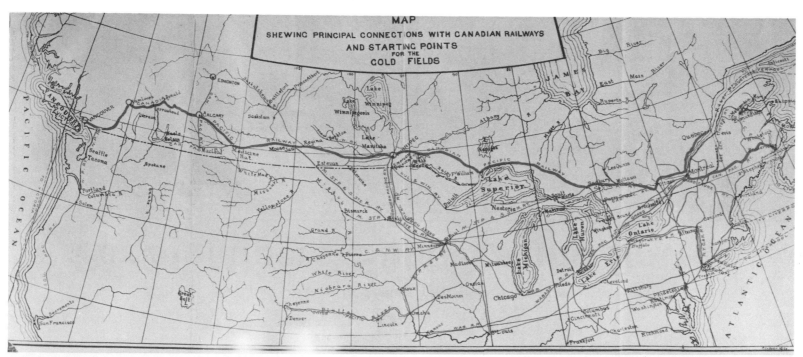

MAP
SHEWING PRINCIPAL CONNECTIONS WITH CANADIAN RAILWAYS
AND STARTING POINTS
FOR THE
GOLD FIELDS

During the winter months one of the best modes of travel available was the dog sled. Although many different adaptations were tried, most miners would revert to the basic dog team and sled. This group, led by Colonel O'Brien, left Edmonton for the Klondike after posing on the bank of the Saskatchewan River just below the Hudson's Bay "Big House" at Fort Edmonton.

62

Some parties of men ventured northward from Edmonton in small groups, using a travois system. This mode of transportation gave each individual the advantage of being independent of his companions.

The B. L. Robinson party left Edmonton in the spring of '98, using horse teams and sleighs for their trip.
Behind them stand the Edmonton Race Track bleachers, which were originally located just north of Main and 103rd Streets.

Since oxen were used extensively in earlier days, it was only natural for some men to choose the animals as their means of transportation to the Klondike. Many drivers used the oxen with the assumption that, when food ran out, the oxen would make a hearty meal. Hence, the caption on this photograph read: "Klondike Beef."

Some Klondikers heading for the gold fields employed the use of home-made sleighs called "jumpers," which were usually pulled by a team of horses.

The Lang party, originally from Ontario, left Edmonton for the gold fields using a Red River cart that once belonged to Louis Riel, and an Indian pony, once the property of Poundmaker. Both are shown in the centre of the photograph.

Ox-carts from eastern Canada were regularly outfitted at Edmonton before continuing on their north-ward trek to Athabasca Landing and the awaiting river transportation. Many of the miners chose oxen for the trip because of their strength and endurance when faced with difficult situations. Note the Union Jack and the U.S. flag on the lead cart.

Prospectors who searched the high mountain ridges and steep gorges for gold relied upon the burro for its sure-footedness.

However, some old-timers took no chances of losing their gear when fording the swiftly flowing creeks of the Far North, and outfitted their animals with life preservers.

This photograph was taken beside Athabasca House, Fort Edmonton.

Excerpt from the Edmonton Bulletin, 1898:

A new and novel way of transporting a Klondike grub stake is introduced by C. L. Smith of Houston, Texas, who will break camp on Tuesday and start with a partner overland via Peace River. The idea is simply three large whiskey barrels packed with the outfit and an iron axle runs through the centre of each one from end to end. The barrels are then placed one after another with a few inches of space between, and the axles of each fastened to a wooden frame. In this order they roll along as an ordinary roller would.

Unfortunately the barrels were not quite as strong as Mr. Smith and his partner anticipated, and just outside of St. Albert the whole contraption fell apart, ending the Texan's journey.

During the summer the most widely used method of transportation was the pack horse. Many an excited group of men, like these on the Groat Estate, set out from Edmonton trailing a long line of overburdened horses behind.

The *Sparrow*, a steamboat equipped with a propeller, was constructed in Edmonton and, according to the advertisements in the Edmonton *Bulletin*, ran trips from Athabasca Landing northward, its maiden voyage being made May 1, 1898.

Ticket and freight agent for the craft was a local businessman named George Jellett.

For the trip from Athabasca Landing northward these four men equipped an old scow with a boiler and canopy, christened it the *Boston* and headed for the gold fields.

Some men had previous sailing experience and could use the northland breezes to best advantage, like this group of five who set out under full sail in a craft named *Jessie*.

For the inventive mind, the waterways gave new ideas a chance to blossom. The Clark party, using an old scow, built a stern wheeler and in the spring of '98 set forth for the Yukon.

Those men with a little more money and a lot more time could always wait at Athabasca Landing for the Hudson's Bay Steamer and buy passage for the trip northward.

This photograph shows what the landing was like in 1896, when the rush had just begun.

Merchants and Their Wares

Because of its geographical position, Edmonton became the main outfitting centre for those men heading north by way of the All Canadian Route. The increased flow of money, and greater business for store owners, led the local merchants to advertise their wares – ranging from medical and food supplies to complete Klondike outfittings. The local newspaper of 1897 wrote: "Interest in the Yukon continues at fever heat, and Edmonton merchants are reaping a tidy harvest from the increased business being done in the town as a result of the influx of people taking the overland route."

A complete miner's outfit, containing both food and clothing, usually cost each man approximately $270, and would sustain him for about one year in the North Country. Since almost two thousand Klondikers were to pass through Edmonton during the rush, the local merchants were not going to lose this choice business, which realized well over half a million dollars.

As always, the Hudson's Bay Company held the leading role as supplier for the majority of the prospectors, but firms like McDougall, Secord, and Ross Brothers Limited stood side by side as leading contenders, matching both price and quality with that offered by the Hudson's Bay Company. As competition was strong, many businesses began the practice of publishing brochures and placing advertisements in the local paper. Some even erected colourful signs and billboards on their store fronts, hoping to entice would-be prospectors to come in and examine their stock.

Prices in Edmonton were very low compared to those in the Yukon, and the miners, knowing this, usually purchased more supplies than were needed in hopes of selling the surplus, for a profit, along the trail. According to the advertisements in the Edmonton *Bulletin*, one could buy heavy woolen shirts at $2.50 each, or high leather boots at $3.50 a pair. Sugar was six and a half cents a pound, tea twenty-five cents, bacon eleven cents, and beans sold at three cents a pound. One old timer even commented that "if a person were able to transport foodstuffs from Edmonton to the Yukon, he could make his fortune without ever leaving the comfort of his store."

However, not all the prospectors' money was spent on food and clothing, for without adequate transportation for his goods a miner could never hope to reach his destination over the rough and rugged trails of the Northland. Hence, during the rush, horses and ox teams were being sold throughout the Edmonton area, as well as down south at Calgary. Since many of the men came from large cities in the East, they were completely helpless when it came to separating the good "beasts of burden," from the bad. Subsequently, many of the greenhorns were sold wild or unbroken horses, and at times Edmonton's Main Street was a mass of bucking broncos and bruised and battered men.

As large parties of men set out for the gold fields during the winter months and early days of spring, John Walter, who owned and operated Walter's Mill, carried out a very profitable business manufacturing sleighs, jumpers and sleds for use along the snow covered trails of the North.

Probably, one of the biggest concerns to any individual contemplating the Yukon trip was the amount of feed necessary to sustain his animals during the long trek. As fodder was by no means scarce in Edmonton, the problem was not one of price but of room, and an ever increasing number of prospectors set out from the town heavily laden with hay for their hard working teams.

Of course there are always the overcautious, who are constantly worried whatever their situation. One such party, under the leadership of a man named O'Brien, brought their own hay with them – all the way from Liverpool, England – as they were not positive whether hay was grown in western Canada and did not want to be caught off guard.

The town's merchants were not only concerned with the outfitting of the many would-be Klondikers passing through Edmonton, but also with the locally based prospectors who worked the Saskatchewan River bars during the late 1890s and early 1900s. These miners, totalling well over nineteen hundred, purchased all their supplies and equipment from the town storehouses. As a result, the banks of the district showed a gold take of over fifty thousand dollars during 1897 alone, from claims staked on the river within the town's limits.

During the gold rush era Edmonton was able to carry on a program of development and expansion – partly due to the influx of money brought in by the Klondikers as well as the local prospecting interests. Many of the town's merchants increased their profits by large margins and, in turn, strengthened the area's prospects for a sound future by reinvesting their gains in the town's economy.

In 1898, the Hudson's Bay Company operated a small trading goods store on Jasper Avenue and 103rd Street, Edmonton.

Here, Klondikers were able to purchase a complete line of supplies before heading northward to the Yukon.

This was the first store in Edmonton to boast a sidewalk.

HUDSON'S BAY STORES
MINERS
COMPLETE OUTFITS
SUPPLIED ON SHORTEST NOTICE

One of the main advantages of the All Canadian Route was its failure to pass through any territory belonging to the United States – all supplies entering the Yukon by this route were classed as duty-free items.

This was usually a strong selling point for the local merchants when advertising their wares, as shown by the cover of this pamphlet.

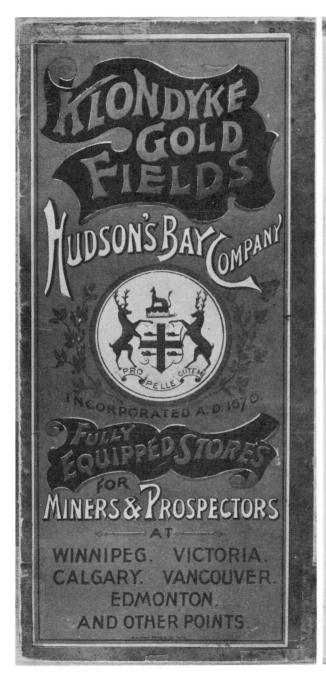

The Hudson's Bay Company distributed a Klondiker's brochure listing in detail the supplies needed by one man for one year in the Klondike country.

25 th Sept 1898

M J Robinson

Bought of The Hudson's Bay Comp.y

Terms, Cash.

Interest will be charged on all overdue Accounts.

1898					
Sept 25	400	Lbs	Flour	10	00
	150	Lbs	Bacon	16	50
	100	Lbs	Navy Beans	4	50
	40	Lbs	Rolled Oats	1	50
	20	Lbs	Corn Meal		75
	10	Lbs	Rice		75
	25	Lbs	Granulated Sugar	1	63
	10	Lbs	Tea	4	00
	20	Lbs	Coffee	8	00
	2	Doz.	Condensed Milk	4	50
	10	Lbs	Baking Powder	5	00
	2	Lbs	Baking Soda		20
	20	Lbs	Salt		40
	20	Lbs	Evaporated Potatoes	5	00
	5	Lbs	Evaporated Onions	2	50
	8	Lbs	Compressed Vegetables	3	25
	1	Lb	Pepper		25
	1/2	Lb	Mustard		25
	1/4	Lb	Evaporated Vinegar		75
	75	Lbs	Evaporated Fruit	10	00
	20	Lbs	Candles	3	20
	6	Tins 4-Oz.	Extract Beef	3	00
	4	Pkg.	Yeast Cakes		40
	1	Pkg.	Tin Matches		75
	1/2	Lb.	Ground Ginger		20
	6	Lbs	Laundry Soap		37
	6	Cakes	Borax or Tar Soap		50
	2	Bottles	Jamaica Ginger		50
	25	Lbs	Hard Tack	2	00
	1	Lb.	Citric Acid		90
				$91	55

Paid H.B.

A MINER'S OUTFIT.

ESTIMATED REQUIREMENTS FOR ONE MAN FOR ONE YEAR.

PROVISIONS.

Apples, evaporated	20 lbs.
Apricots, "	15 "
Bacon	200 "
Baking powder	10 "
Barley, pot	10 "
Beans	100 "
Beef extract	1 doz.
Candles	25 lbs.
Coffee	10 "
Corn Meal	20 "
Flour	500 "
Lime juice	1 gal.
Matches	5 boxes
Milk, condensed	1 doz.
Mustard	1 lb.
Oats, rolled	50 "
Peas, split	10 "
Pepper	1 "
Prunes	10 "
Rice	25 "
Salt	20 "
Soap	10 "
Soda, baking	2 "
Sugar	75 "
Tea, compressed	10 "
Tobacco, smoking	10 "
Vegetables, compressed	12 "
Yeast Cakes	3 doz.

CLOTHING.

Blankets	2 pairs
Cap, cloth	1 only
Cap, fur	1 "
Coats, corduroy lined or buckskin	1 "
" Oilskin	1 "
Dunnage Bag	1 "
Gloves, skin	1 pair
" wool	1 "
Goggles, snow	1 "
Handkerchiefs, colored	1 doz.
Mitts, leather	1 pair
Mitts, wool	2 "
Mosquito netting	10 yds.
Overalls	2 pairs
Pants, moleskin	1 "
Sheet, ground	1 only
Shirts, flannel	3 only
" mackinaw	1 "
Socks, wool	12 pairs
Suspenders	1 pair
Sweaters, wool	2 only
Towels,	1 doz.
Underwear, wool	3 suits

FOOTWEAR.

Boots, laced	2 pair
Boots, rubber	1 "
Duffles	2 "
Moccasins,	3 "
Socks, long Arctic	2 "
Snow shoes	1 "

HARDWARE.

Auger	1 only
Axe, chopping	1 "
Brace and bits	1 set
Camp kettles	1 nest
Chisel	1 only
Coffee pot	1 "
Compass, pocket	1 "
Cup, tin	1 "
Knife, butcher's	1 "
Knife and fork	1 "
Files	3 "
Fry pan	1 "
Gold pan	1 "
Hammer	1 "
Hatchet	1 "
Nails, assorted	20 lbs.
Oakum	10 "
Picks, miner's	2 only
Pick handles	3 "
Pitch	10 lbs.
Plates, tin	2 only
Rope	25 lbs.
Saw, hand	1 only
" whip	1 "
Saw set	1 "
Scales, gold	1 set
Screw driver	1 only
Shovels, miner's	2 "
Spoons, assorted	3 "

Approximate cost of above outfit (subject to market fluctuations) will be :

at
WINNIPEG
CALGARY
EDMONTON
VANCOUVER
and
VICTORIA

From $190 to $220, according to the point at which purchased.

FOR PARTIES, the cost per man can be diminished according to numbers, as several of the articles can be used in common.

TENTS AND ANY OTHER REQUIREMENTS can be supplied according to the season for travelling and route selected.

During the gold rush era the Hudson's Bay Company still maintained a supply store within the confines of Fort Edmonton, in conjunction with their general store on Edmonton's Main Street. This photograph shows Fort Edmonton as it appeared in 1896.

This small party of gold seekers posed in front of the Athabasca Building – inside the stockade at Fort Edmonton – after securing their supplies from the storehouse.

Here the Davis party are shown, after purchasing some additional supplies, in front of what photographer Ernest Brown calls Johnstone Walker's first store in Edmonton.

At the time of the gold rush, John A. McDougall, a former independent trader, operated a very profitable business in Edmonton as a general merchant. His store was located on the north side of what is now Jasper Avenue, between 101st Street and 102nd Street. This photo shows a group of Klondikers fully outfitted, about to depart for the North using pack horses.

Robert Secord, a local fur trader and land buyer, owned the property adjoining that of John McDougall. In 1897 the two firms joined forces in an effort to improve their services to the local population as well as to the Klondikers passing through the town.

For many years, Walter's Mill, on the south bank of the Saskatchewan River, was one of the town's leading industries. During the gold rush era it supplied many a prospector with his means of transportation to the gold fields. Insert: an advertisement from the Edmonton *Bulletin*, dated 1898.

Medical supplies were sold by many firms and ranged in price from a few cents for the necessary basics up to ten dollars for a complete miner's first-aid kit. The primary contents always contained snow-blindness remedies and frost-bite cures. All were commonly dehydrated to prevent damage or loss by freezing.

A Model Medicine Chest.

We would advise all persons who contemplate going to the Klondyke region to include in their outfits a medicine chest containing the following drugs, the cost of which should be within $10:

Quinine pills	50
Compound cathartic pills	50
Acetanilid tablets	3 dozen
Chlorate potash	1 box
Mustard plasters	6
Belladonna plasters	6
Carbolic salve	4 ounces
Chloroform liniment	8 ounces
Witch hazel	1 pint
Essence ginger	4 ounces
Paregoric	4 ounces
Laudanum	1 ounce
Borax	4 ounces
Tincture iodine	1 ounce
Spirits of nitre	2 ounces
Tincture of iron	1 ounce
Cough mixture	8 ounces
Toothache drops	1 bottle
Vaseline	1 bottle
Iodoform	2 drams
Lint	2 yards
Assorted bandages	½ dozen
Rubber adhesive plasters	2 feet
Absorbent cotton	4 ounces

Monsell's salts for hemorrhages—In quantities in accordance with the person's liability to attacks of the trouble.

George Graydon was Edmonton's first druggist and began his practice in a small apothecary's shop near what is now Jasper Avenue and 98th Street. Many of the men heading north obtained their medical supplies from the wide selection in his store. For many years Graydon was the official North West Mounted Police druggist, and well known and respected for his work.

In 1898, a small pocket-size booklet entitled *The Little Nugget* was distributed in Edmonton. Within its pages a prospector could find the answers to all his questions regarding the gold fields.

Of great interest to most miners was Chapter III of the booklet, outlining a complete list of articles necessary for a Klondike expedition.

CHAPTER III.

WHAT TO TAKE WITH YOU.

List of Articles Necessary for a Complete Outfit for a Klondyke Expedition.

Articles.	Weight, Lbs.	Cost.
Clothing	65	$75

Two suits heavy underwear, 6 pairs heavy woolen stockings, 2 pairs blanket lined mittens, 1 heavy mackinaw coat, 2 pairs mackinaw trousers, 2 dark woolen overshirts, 1 heavy sweater, 1 heavy rubber lined top coat, 2 pairs heavy rubber boots, or arctic overshoes with felt leggins, 2 pairs shoes, 1 Canadian snow-shoeing cap, 1 pair extra heavy blankets, 1 suit oil clothing, 2 pairs overalls, needles, thread, beeswax, and towels.

Groceries	590	50

Three hundred and fifty pounds of flour, 150 pounds of bacon, 50 pounds of beans, 10 pounds of tea, 5 pounds of baking powder, 50 pounds of salt, 25 pounds dried fruit, 25 pounds of desiccated vegetables, 5 pounds of soap, 1 tin of matches, ½ pound of saccharine.

Hardware	70	$50

One long-handled shovel, 1 pick, 1 ax, 5 pounds of wire nails, 5 pounds of pitch, 3 pounds of oakum, 2 large files, hammer, brace-and-bit, large whipsaw, 150 feet ⅝-inch rope, drawknife, chisel, scythe, stone, shaving outfit, cooking utensils, 2 buckets, and gold pan.

Armament	40	29

One repeating rifle, 40-82, with reloading tools and 100 rounds of brass-shell cartridges, 1 large hunting knife, and an assortment of fishing tackle.

Camping outfit	30	20

One heavy canvas tent, 8x10, 1 heavy canvas sleeping bag, 1 sheet-iron stove, made in collapsible form, and with telescopic pipe; guy and peg ropes for tent.

Totals	795	$224

Cost and weight of outfit and expense of transportation can be materially reduced by prospectors traveling in groups of three or four, as one camping, hardware, and armament rig will answer for two men. In traveling by steamer or rail, 150 pounds of baggage is checked free for each passenger.

Throughout 1898 most of the major stores and businesses placed advertisements in the Edmonton *Bulletin* telling of their wares and services:

Ross Brothers Limited, situated near what is now Jasper Avenue and 100th Street, advertised low cost, complete Klondike supplies for the would-be prospector.

For the man travelling in the North Country it was a must to wear the proper clothing, and many miners obtained their goods from the firm of Larue and Picard on Edmonton's Main Street.

Even the local insurance company set up special life insurance policies which were readily available to all prospectors at low annual rates.

Edmonton and Her Gold

Edmonton's first contact with gold fever came in 1862[1], when a former school teacher named Clover panned the Saskatchewan River near what is the present site of Clover Bar. From that time on, men began to search the sand and gravel beds of the river from Fort Saskatchewan to Big Island, and it is said that, in all, over nineteen hundred men could be seen at one time or another using "grizzlies," "cradles" and "rockers" along the shores of the river.

According to early editions of the Edmonton *Bulletin*, over a series of years beginning about 1894, the river yielded more than three million dollars in gold dust to those miners hardy enough to take its treasure. Unfortunately, most of these first prospectors have long since been forgotten, and names like those of Sam Livingstone and James Gibbons, who were among the first to work the sands, are now only brief, faded lines in the early editions of the local newspaper.

In 1897, when the rush was in full swing, the *Bulletin* published numerous stories about Edmonton and her gold, including this report dealing with the citizens of the town:

> The favorite occupation around town now is staking mining claims. Numerous parties have been leaving lately at strange hours of the night, all laden with mining equipment and bent on getting ahead of each other. The river is reported to be staked sixty miles up.

The methods employed by these early prospectors were, until later years, as simplified as possible, and usually of three basic types: "placer," "rocker" or "cradle" and "sluicing."

Placer, or poor man's mining as it was often called, was used extensively on the Saskatchewan during the late 1890s and early 1900s and, as it employed no machinery or costly apparatus, the technique was simple enough for all to undertake. When a likely location was found, the miner would clean away the coarse gravel and loose stones from the area and place the underlying fine sand into a broad, shallow pan: he then proceeded to fill the pan with water and slowly "work" the fine sand out, leaving only the heavier gold flecks, intermingled with a few remaining traces of sand, behind. The contents of the pan were dumped into a wooden barrel containing water and a pound or two of mercury. When the gold came in contact with the mercury the two combined, leaving the sand separate and suspended in the water.

This gold-mercury formation was then taken from the barrel and placed in a thin, porous buckskin

[1] In 1862 a group of approximately 250 individuals from Upper and Lower Canada passed through the Fort Edmonton area on a trip from Fort Garry to the Cariboo gold rush region. This was the largest organized trek west prior to the coming of the railway, and as the route used was by land the party were called the "Overlanders."

bag which was squeezed and twisted, forcing the mercury through its walls and leaving the gold, containing a small amount of mercury, behind. The gold was then retrieved through a process called "roasting" or "firing," which involved heating the remaining mixture until the mercury evaporated, leaving behind the pure gold. This method, however, was never utilized for any length of time, due to its slowness in comparison to other methods which were popular at the time, and eventually placer mining was employed only as a means of finding a suitable area to work.

A more profitable method of retrieving gold was with the use of a "rocker" or "cradle," which was simply an oblong box approximately three feet in length and two feet in width. It was constructed of two parts: a top section – shallow with a bottom track of heavy sheet iron – which had a great series of one-quarter inch holes evenly spaced throughout; and a lower section with the same dimensions as the top, but having an inclined plane about half way down its depth, over which was placed a heavy woolen blanket. The whole apparatus was then set on two rockers which, as on a baby's cradle, worked with a side-to-side rocker motion.

After a suitable location was found, the prospector would take time to gather the sand and gravel into a large mound from which he could easily fill his rocker without having to relocate the cumbersome apparatus every few days. The upper section would be filled with sand and gravel, and at the same time a steady flow of water would be directed over it. When the cradle was rocked, the result would be that the finer material, containing the gold dust, would fall through the one-quarter-inch holes and onto the inclined plane and woolen blanket. As the gold particles were heavier than the particles of sand, they would imbed themselves in the blanket, while the debris would be washed away. The nuggets, because of their larger size, were held by the upper box ensuring for the prospector little or no loss of his valuable gold. As an additional check, at the base of the inclined plane were tiny slats or depressions which held a small amount of mercury and served to catch any gold that happened to be washed past the blanket by the water.

Although both placer and rocker mining were popular, most individuals preferred a method commonly known as "sluicing." Using this procedure, up to three times the amount of gold could be extracted from the sands, compared to the yields retrieved by other widely employed methods. Unfortunately, one of the basic requirements for sluicing was a large, constant flow of water. In many cases this alone prevented its application, as only near bodies of water could sluicing be carried out.

A long trough or chute was constructed, forming a basic apparatus similar to a rectangular box.

This was then equipped with many small slats or shallow depressions along the bottom of its track, and in these were placed small amounts of mercury. The procedure then taken was similar to that of the rocker method, in that a large stock pile of sand and gravel was built up near the working area and was constantly thrown into the trough. However, the sluice box was not rocked. Instead, a steady, swift-flowing stream of water quickly washed all the material over the small slats or depressions, allowing the heavier gold to sink and lie trapped within the series of mercury pockets along the sluice box's track.

It was inevitable that, as the Saskatchewan continued to give up her gold and as technology advanced, an entirely new method of gold retrieval would emerge. This came in the form of huge mechanical dredges, similar to those used before this period in Australia, New Zealand and eastern Canada for mining and seaport clearing projects.

These units, many weighing well over three tons, were built mainly in the yards of Walter's Mill under the strict supervision of a man named Hobson whose trade was originally the building of sea dredges for coastal work.

The great advantage of these machines was their ability to obtain from the river bed large amounts of gold-laden material, using suction pipes, buckets or conveyor belts, then sluicing out the material for its riches.

However, the dredges did have one serious disadvantage in that their mechanical parts were so numerous and cumbersome that it was almost impossible to tell whether the dredge was in need of repair until it broke down completely, usually damaging various other parts in the process.

From the time the first dredges touched the waters of the Saskatchewan River, in 1894, the Edmonton *Bulletin* kept regular accounts of their progress and published the name of each new dredging craft as it was pressed into action. Throughout the paper would appear such names as *Gold Pan*, *Potter's*, *Notre Dame de Mistassini*, *Jubilee*, *Otter*, et cetera. The paper was also quick to announce the owners of each new dredge, many of whom were prominent citizens of the area: Jenner, Braithwaite, Potter, Frazer, Levey, Osborne, Burke and Bell were just a few of the many names recorded in the *Bulletin*.

In the Sessional Papers of the third session of the eighth Parliament in Ottawa, dated 1898, the annual report of Superintendent A. H. Griesbach, commander of the "G" Division of the North West Mounted Police and in charge of the Edmonton area, contained the following account of the gold involvement in this region:

During the season, besides the usual "Grizzly" workers, there have been in operation, upon the Saskatchewan River, 12 dredges of various construction, some worked by steam, some by horse power, others by hand, these dredges, with one or two exceptions have made good pay, but it is impossible to give any figures as regards the quantities taken out by them, as each dredge owner claimed that he had a "Klondike," in his machine, and they all were very reticent about giving any figures, but it is sufficient to say that they are all going to work again next spring with improved machinery, etc.

A mining syndicate from Nebraska was operating a "Concentrator" during the latter part of the summer on a bar about three miles above Fort Saskatchewan. Their machinery, consisting of three concentrating tables, separators, etc., was set up on the sand and was worked by electricity, the intention being to experiment during the summer, and if the result of the experiments reached their expectations they intend starting again in the spring. The result evidently was satisfactory, as their managing director stated on leaving here that he would be back again in the spring with improved machinery, and would build a boat and commence operations.

During the early spring the residents of that part of this district bordering on the Saskatchewan River were put in a state of mild excitement owing to the fact that the "black sand" lying upon the edges of the banks and on the bottom of the river was found to be more or less valuable, some process having been discovered by which it can be successfully washed. A great number of claims were staked. The excitement has somewhat abated but will, no doubt, arise again upon the advent of spring.

As gold dredging increased, it became necessary to name many of the river bars and tributaries to distinguish where each claim was situated. Hence, new names began to appear: Bernard's Slough, Hibbert's Bar, MacDonald's Bar, Gold Island and Saddle Creek.

With the advent of the gold dredge there came the capitalists and profit makers to organize and promote new dredging syndicates. Most of these syndicates were backed by stockholders in the United States or eastern Canada and sold their shares at one dollar each, par value. However, in some cases the backer was a local businessman, like Edmonton's Issac Cowie, who founded the Victoria-Alberta Gold Dredging Syndicate in the early days of Edmonton's rush for the yellow metal. In the late 1890s new companies were beginning to form in great numbers. Looking over the town's old records, one spots such names as The Star Mining Company and The Platinum Dredging Syndicate from London, England

– both quite successful.

The costs involved in setting up a dredging company, even in those days, were fantastically high, and before embarking on a venture such as this careful investigations were carried out. The following is a direct quote from the files of the Saskatchewan Gold and Platinum Proprietary Limited regarding their estimated costs and profits:

It is estimated that the average gold of the submerged bed of the Saskatchewan River, in the localities covered by these cases, is on a conservative estimate one hundred thousand dollars per mile. The value of thirty miles at that rate is three million dollars.

The cost of dredging and saving the gold per mile is estimated to be ten thousand dollars, that per thirty miles is three hundred thousand dollars, which deducted from three million dollars would leave a balance of two million, seven hundred thousand dollars for the general expenses of management and profit.

With gold dredges on the river and prospectors on the shores, the Saskatchewan's gold rush lived on until 1907, when the last of the old-timers finally died or gave up their search for riches. However, as the Saskatchewan's gold is thought to come not from one main source, but a great many small pockets, the old miners often said that the gold would never be depleted, but continually build up to await another rush for the precious metal.

The traditional method of "panning" for gold was a common sight in the Edmonton area, as well as on the many claims along the Yukon streams of the North.

The "grizzly," an adaptation of the common sluice box, was used extensively during the late 1800s and was considered much more efficient than other manual retrieval methods employed up to that time.

This photograph shows the type of "rocker" or "cradle" often used on the Saskatchewan River by the early prospectors. The adaptation of the handles and the wheel enabled the prospector to use the apparatus as a wheelbarrow when gathering sand and gravel for processing.

A group of men near the present site of the High Level Bridge, using a grizzly. With this method over $50,000 was taken from the river in the summer of 1896.

A gold dredge at work on the Saskatchewan River. Note the amount of water needed to wash the sand and gravel clean of its gold. Even in the 1900s the estimate of salvageable gold averaged over fifty cents a yard when using a dredge capable of obtaining sand from the river bed to a depth of eighteen feet.

This dredge, although smaller than most, was owned and operated by a Dr. Braithwaite and was quite successful working on Hibbert's bar, until demolished in the river flood of 1898. Many dredges of this type were manually operated.

Many of the dredges used near Edmonton were built at Walter's Mill under the guidance of a Mr. Hobson and varied greatly in construction. Jenner's gold dredge, the *Jubilee*, employed a "dipper" or "bucket" attached to the front of the craft to scoop up the gravel for washing.

138

A gold dredge at work using a conveyor-belt system. These dredges operated up to twenty-four buckets on each belt and as a result were able to collect sand and gravel much faster than it could be processed.

During the winter months many gold dredges were put into drydock to await the coming of spring and the thawing of the river ice. This photograph was taken near the end of Edmonton's gold era, about 1907.

The suction gold dredge employed the use of a large "sucker" to obtain the gold-laden gravel of the river bed. Here, one of the owners stands beside a submerged "sucker pipe." These craft weighed well over three tons and were busily working the river bed as early as 1896.

For many, the advent of the winter months only forecast a slight slowing down of mining operations, or a change in mining methods.

On August 21, 1895, Bishop Grandin and two assistants pronounced a blessing over a new gold dredge called the *Notre Dame de Mistassini*. On August 18, 1899, she ran aground during a sudden flood and was completely destroyed.

This photo was taken in the spring of 1899 when the Saskatchewan River flooded, taking with it the main river ferry and many of the gold-dredging machines in the Edmonton area.

As gold dredges proved very successful, adaptations were continually being made on existing models in order to improve on their efficiency. This drawing shows a dredge patented by a man named Hebert who came to Edmonton from Ontario in the early days of the gold rush.

152

The Under-water adjustable Gold mining machine.

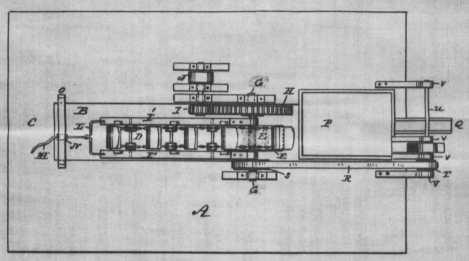

Fig. 1.

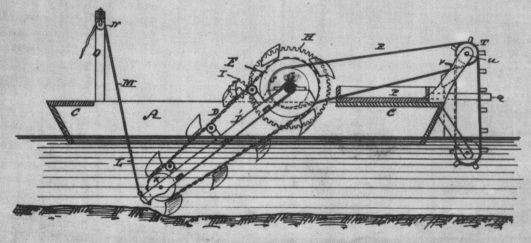

Fig. 2.

Many of the prospectors built small one-room shacks near their claims in order to enforce their rights and prevent claimjumpers from causing any trouble. As a rule, the only company they had was when a river boat on a Sunday sightseeing trip, up the Saskatchewan, would stop near them to take on additional fuel.

When the gold panning was poor, they were able to supplement their income by cutting cordwood for the Hudson's Bay steamers and, in exchange, were given credit at the store.

In the days before the construction of Edmonton's Low Level Bridge, most prospectors' supplies crossed the Saskatchewan River by way of the Upper and Lower Ferries. Although quite slow, this was essentially the only connection between the towns of Edmonton and Strathcona.

In September 1912 His Royal Highness The Duke of Connaught officially opened the galleries of the Alberta Parliament Buildings to the public. For this occasion a golden key made with gold washed from the Saskatchewan River was used.

On October 21, 1897, a group of eleven businessmen from the Edmonton area signed a partnership agreement forming a gold mining company known as the "Clatworthy Prospecting Association." Their main objective was "to proceed to the Klondike gold fields to prospect for and work gold, and other minerals and precious stones."

The men involved were: E. A. Harris, William J. Austin, L. C. Rolt, T. F. Truman, Thomas Clatworthy, A. C. Hervey, Clayton Freeling, Frank H. Bennett, H. Stephens, Albert E. Moloney and John Francis. Each man was required to pay a subscription fee of two hundred pounds.

This photograph shows the plan of their Edmonton camp and is taken from an original drawing dated January 4, 1898.

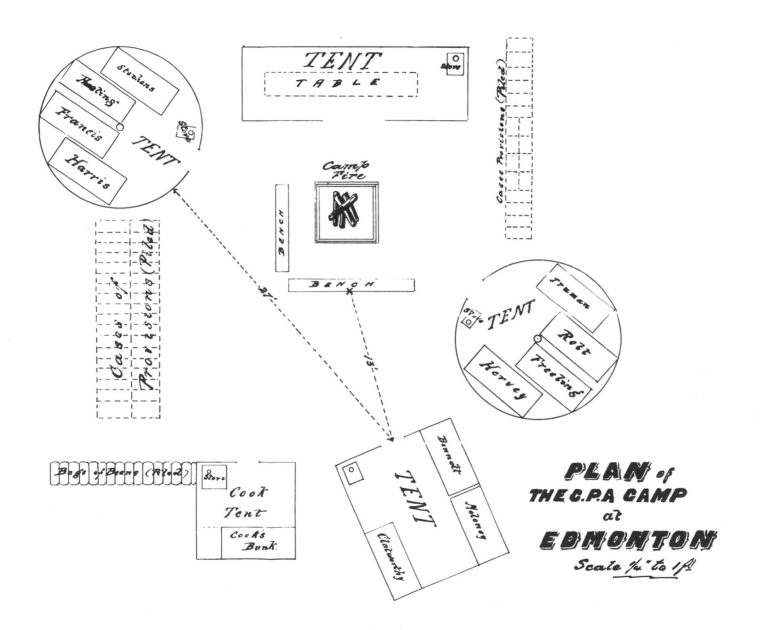

PLAN of
THE C.P.A. CAMP
at
EDMONTON
Scale ¼" to 1ft.

The Golden Era

It would be impossible to list the many people who took part in the gold rush era of Edmonton, or the trek to the Yukon gold fields via the All Canadian Route. Their names have long since ceased to be remembered and now lie almost forgotten within the record vaults of local government offices.

These hardy prospectors were of a breed quite similar to Canada's early settlers in that they were striving for a new start in life, and perhaps it was the call of danger, uncertainty and hopeful dreams that gave them the impetus to endure the hardships and sorrows they were to face. Cold and hunger, disease and death were commonplace to them, and were accepted as natural hazards of their environment.

The lure of gold affected not only the seasoned miners, but also attracted the women, the young and the old alike. The inexperienced came in hopes of mingling with the experienced, while the old-timers came with the idea of beating the "greenhorns," and other "sourdoughs" to the awaiting riches. Many came with high spirits, only to leave completely broke and disheartened. Others were much more fortunate – they made their fortune within a few months' time and returned home to find fame and glory awaiting them. All in all, everyone even remotely connected with the gold rush felt the effects of its power, both good and bad.

The gold-seekers of the 1890s could be classed in three separate groups, each with their own distinct characteristics, and dependent upon each other for survival.

The majority were ordinary people searching for easy riches and a comfortable living, as the depression prior to the rush had left many of them with scars and painful memories of the past. Of the hundreds of individuals who came in search of gold, these people were without a doubt the most excited and hopeful of the lot.

Many were labourers from the large cities in eastern Canada and the United States, or fresh off homesteads and used to hard work and long, tiring hours. Some had the good fortune to have had previous experience in the gold mining business, during the California and British Columbia gold booms; but most were completely ignorant of proper mining methods and came from their homes with no more than a strong will and an eager heart. Perhaps it was just as well these people knew nothing of what lay before them. If they had, many would-be prospectors might never have ventured from their homes, regardless of the conditions they were facing there.

The following poem, entitled "The Song of the Klondyke," was published in a prospector's handbook of 1898, and probably depicts better than any prose the dreams and hopes each Klondiker held for the future:

All you miners, wide awake!
Go to the Klondyke; make your stake.
Get out your pick, your pan, your pack,
Ho, for the Klondyke, ho!

There's gold enough for you and me,
On the hill and the plain, wherever you be;
And it's yellow and rich, and heavy as lead,
But half of the truth has never been said.
Ho, for the Klondyke, ho!

No man there has ever been broke,
And there's gold enough for the women folk;
And the nights are short when the days are long;
So pack your tools and sing this song:
Ho, for the Klondyke, ho!

CHORUS

Ho, for the Klondyke,
Ho, for the Klondyke,
Ho, for the Klondyke, ho!

Put on your pack
And don't come back
Till you fill your sack
On the Northwest track.
Ho, ho, for the Klondyke, ho!

164

The profit makers and commercial businessmen constituted the second class of people to be drawn by the lure of gold. With the increased rate of mining activities, both in the Edmonton area and the Yukon, came a greater need for supplies and services. Hence, many men expanded their businesses hoping to cash in, not only on the local demands, but also those of the northern areas. A large number of new companies also were formed, within the town as well as in places as far away as Montreal and New York. Some of these businesses, like the Good Hope Mining Company and the Montreal Mining Company, set out for the North by way of the All Canadian Route through Edmonton, after purchasing their supplies from the McDougall and Secord stores.

The companies that went bankrupt within the space of a few months were, by far, in the majority; but some of the more enterprising men were able to hold on to their investments and develop the companies' assets to such an extent that within a few years they were able to sell out to larger firms and retire, never again to worry about their financial outlook.

The last class of would-be prospectors were of a sort commonly referred to as "adventurers" or "vagabonds," and made up the smallest group of individuals to travel to the North in search of golden riches. Most were young men eager to make their fortune and return home again and did not fancy the idea of working too hard in order to obtain their share of the gold. Many of these men came from the United States by way of the railroad and travelled the route to Edmonton, or beyond, in search of fortune and fame. Of these men very little is known, for they were continually drifting from one place to another, usually just one step ahead of the law or one step behind those miners lucky enough to strike it rich.

During the first days of the gold rush the men and women who chose to travel the route from Edmonton were somewhat at a loss, for the town had few lodging places of any size apart from the Edmonton Hotel, built in 1871, and operated by Donald Ross. Later, however, another hotel was constructed near the east end of what is now Jasper Avenue. Although its name was simply "Big Hotel," it became one of Edmonton's most colourful and historic landmarks during the Klondike era. Shortly after it was built, an ex-prospector named Gibbons purchased the establishment and changed its name to "Columbia House." It is said that the miners often sat on its steps to rest and chew the fat with their comrades. During the fall months many of the men would patiently stare out the hotel windows waiting for freeze-up, so that they might begin their long journey to the Yukon.

In 1898 Jim Delaney, one of Edmonton's better known prospectors, arrived back from the North

Country after one of his many gold mining trips and began a celebration that later became known throughout the country as "Delaney's Drunk." After obtaining a room in the Columbia House, Jim set about purchasing a large steer, which he promptly barbecued in the middle of Main Street, and invited many of his friends to the feast. The party, it is said, lasted all night long and by morning the only ones remaining were Delaney and a few of his Indian friends. He then packed his gear and left once again for the Far North. This colourful character eventually retired and moved up north to live, taking with him a photograph of Columbia House and many memories of the "Good Years."

In the later days of the gold rush a number of new hotels and rooming houses had been built and, looking through the town directory, one finds the names of such hotels as the Grand Central, the Windsor and the St. Elmo. Rooming houses had increased also and sported eye-catching names like: The White House, American Boarding House, Gold Boarding House and the Bonaventure.

Many of the miners and prospectors on their way northward from farther south stayed in these hotels and rooming houses while being outfitted. Their names still rest, yellowed and faded with age, upon the registers of each establishment. Other individuals, however, were better remembered and their names still appear from time to time in various publications.

For a great number of years local newspapers and historians have noted that Robert Service, poet and world traveller, had resided in the Edmonton area prior to the Yukon Rush of '98, and from there, in the late 1890s left for the North Country. There have also been many individuals who have connected themselves or their relatives with the mythical characters portrayed in the poems of Robert Service.

But, according to Robert Service's brother, Dr. Stanley Service, all this is untrue. Throughout his lifetime, Robert Service never once visited Edmonton, although his family had lived here for some time. The closest he ever came to the town was a three-month holiday in the Manville area where his parents operated a small farm. The individuals created within his poems were nothing more than composites of the many people he had met throughout his travels. "The lady that's known as Lou," who for many years was thought to be a local celebrity, was nothing more than a creature of the poet's imagination. Quoting directly from correspondence received from Dr. Service:

Robert did not live in Edmonton at any time prior to going to the Yukon or after. My mother, two brothers and myself lived there for about twelve years. Robert did not visit us during that time.

Robert left the Bank where he worked in Scotland in 1895 at the age of twenty-one to come to

166

Canada to learn farming and wander about the country in general. In 1903 he joined the Bank of Commerce in Vancouver and was sent to Vancouver Island. He was then transferred to the White Horse Bank in about 1905. He was there for three years and wrote his first poems. He then had three months holidays and spent it with us at our farm near Manville, Alberta. . . .

"The lady that's known as Lou"; He told me she was a composite character, not one individual; the same applies to Sam McGee and Dan McGrew. I asked him about these characters when he visited us for three weeks on his last trip to Canada. Many people telephone and ask these questions and in some cases identify their relatives or themselves with them. Robert just laughed and said to me: "It is too bad to puncture the bubble. . . ."

Another individual who should receive recognition for the part she played in the quest for gold is Mrs. Garner, the first woman to leave Edmonton for the Yukon using the All Canadian Route. In August of 1897, on a chilly but bright summer morning, she left town – much to the amazement of many of the local citizens, for this was one year before the great mass of men passed through the area late in 1898. The fact that a woman was going to use the virtually unknown trail brought a surge of mixed emotions to the townsfolk. Some called it disastrous and foolhardy, while others felt it a brave and courageous gesture and an example of the endurance and stamina of the women of that period.

Although more is known about those people who headed northward over the trail than those who remained in Edmonton to seek their fortune, this does not alter the fact that many men did indeed prospect and mine the river which flows through Edmonton. Their names appear throughout the pages of this book and were more important to the economy of Edmonton than most people realize. From the gold panner and sluice-box worker to the gold dredger and syndicate executive, all were commonplace in the town from the early 1890s until 1907, and to a large extent helped in its development both locally and throughout Western Canada.

C. W. Mathers, Edmonton's first photographer, was responsible for recording on film the early history of the Edmonton area and the Far North. Included in his works are the majority of the photographs covering the gold era and its effects on the region surrounding Edmonton.

Ernest Brown, successor to Mathers, began his career in 1903 and for over forty years carried on the fine photographic tradition, with the help of Miss Gladys Reeves.

Robert Service – poet, historian, and world traveller. His works relating to the Klondike are known by all ages and, although he never lived in the Edmonton area, his family resided in the city for many years. It was in this cabin that he created his many mythical characters, and wrote his first book of poems.

170

Jim Delaney was one of Edmonton's better known prospectors. Here he poses on what is now Jasper Avenue in front of the Columbia House. After celebrating his return from the North by throwing a huge party, which lasted the entire night and included the barbecuing of a whole steer on Main Street, he returned to the North Country. This little episode later became known as "Delaney's Drunk."

Mrs. Garner, the first lady to head for the Klondike via the All Canadian Route, left Edmonton in August 1897. Her departure created an uproar in town as the trail had just opened and even the hardy prospectors were somewhat leery of the conditions which one might encounter along the route during the cold fall months.

These photographs show two types of men, each lured northward by hopes of great wealth. Mr. M. Crews, with his long hair and broad-brimmed hat, is the typical adventurer of the 1890s, always moving from one place to another. Mr. Hastings, on the other hand, typifies the average, ordinary gold seeker, looking for a more comfortable living and freedom from debt and insecurity. These photos were taken in The Mathers Studio, Edmonton.

Two of the most prosperous groups to work the waters of the Saskatchewan River were the Jenner party and the Potter party. Both held claims on dredging equipment during the late 1890s, and did very well.

The would-be gold miners of the late 1890s came from all walks of life, and Edmonton's photographer C. W. Mathers managed to capture portraits of many of them before they headed north to the Yukon or began their work on the sand bars of the Saskatchewan River.

Left to right, beginning with the top row: Denhardt, Abel and Hall group, Ralt brothers
Center: Robertson party
Bottom Row: Lutitt party, Hardfield party, Jackson party

This photograph of the National Klondike Mining and Trading Company shows the type of interest that began to emerge as the wealth of the gold began to show in the country's economy. These men travelled to Edmonton from eastern Canada in an effort to reach the gold fields of the Yukon by way of the All Canadian Route.

182

As most of the prospectors were wholly dependent upon animals for their transportation, blacksmith shops, harness companies and livery stables were able to expand into profitable enterprises. New establishments began to spring up overnight throughout the town's business section. The H. A. Finch Company, Edmonton's first livery stable, worked in healthy competition with the Eclipse Stables, Al Brown's Livery and the McCauley Livery and Feed Stables.

The Jasper House, where many miners stayed, was built, just before the gold rush, on the north side of Main Street. It boasted of being not only the largest public house in the area, but also the only hotel to be constructed of brick. Its proprietor was a man named Goodridge.

The Grand Central Hotel, owned and operated by a Mr. Moller and Mr. Reinhold Matz, was doing a good business in the years prior to 1900, and according to an excerpt from the Edmonton *Bulletin:* "The surge of Yukon bound prospectors, which flooded through Edmonton in 1899, added its quota to the Hotel's thriving trade."

The Alberta Hotel saw the coming and going of a great many prospectors. One not-so-pleasant account is recorded in the judicial files of the Supreme Court of the Northwest Territories, Edmonton, dated 1898. The case is between the proprietors of the hotel, Mr. Alfred Jackson and Mr. Del Grierson, and the members of the Alaska Mining and Trade Company, 204 Dearborn Street, Chicago, U.S.A.

It appears that the company (registered in Illinois as a general mining, smelting, and manufacturing company) took room, board and livery stable benefits while in Edmonton, and before heading north, but unfortunately failed to pay their bill of $343.08 when they left.

Without a past,
We have no hope of a future.
Without a future,
We have no need of a past.
                    Jim Blower

Credits

Acknowledgements

I would like to express my thanks to all who
have helped make this publication possible:

Linda Blower
Alma Brundige
Tom Court
William Edgar
Karl Kaesekamp
Esther Kreisel
The Honourable Grant MacEwan
Jane Mathers
Mr. and Mrs. Edward McDougall
Roman Ostashewsky
Gladys Reeves
Allan Ridge
Dr. Stanley Service.
The City of Edmonton
Hudson's Bay Archives
Provincial Museum and Archives of Alberta
Public Archives, Ottawa
Royal Canadian Mounted Police Museum
University of Washington, Seattle.

J.B.